Eyelight Poems

From my heart to yours
Acrossspace and time.
Peace and love–
Ken

Eyelight Poems

Ken Fox

BERKELEY, CALIFORNIA / 2003

Copyright © 2003 by Rose Esther Fox
All rights reserved
Printed in the United States of America

Published by
Whitewing Press, Tucson, Arizona

Library of Congress Control Number: 20033106701
ISBN 1-888965-04-5

The poem on the back cover is reprinted from *The Long
Road Turns to Joy: A Guide to Walking Meditation* (1996) by
Thich Nhat Hanh, with permission of Parallax Press,
Berkeley, California, www.parralax.org.

Foreword

KEN FOX DIED ON MAY 7, 2001, after a twelve-year coura-
geous battle with prostate cancer. Ken was a gentle,
powerful and passionate man whose life I was blessed to
share for fifty years. He was a political activist and an
advocate for children and all wildlife and nature. He was
a man of fathomless creativity, leaving behind him a
wealth of unpublished written work as well as music
compositions. He was also a teacher and an intuitive
therapist remembered by his clients and students whom
he encouraged to follow their own dreams, as he had
done. Only the last stages of his illness could finally stop
his words and the sound of his classical melodies. He
never took the time to prepare any of his creations for
publication. He was always too busy exploring the next
melody, the next essay or letter of protest, the next poem,
or the next challenge.

His death left a silence that no other words or sounds can
replace, for he was a rare and talented human being. He
would have been 79 on July 7, 2003. I did not want

another day to pass without making a very small sample of his writing available to those of us who knew and loved him, and for those who might get to know him through his poetry.

I want to thank Rebecca Salome, my editor and creative mentor for interrupting her busy life to prepare this book on very short notice. It could not have happened without her. My gratitude goes also to Harrison Shaffer, for designing the book. Last but not least, I want to thank Andy Stewart for preparing the cover photo, which was actually taken by Ken's son, Bill, as well as the snapshot of Ken that appears on the back of the book.

—*Ken's Rose*

About the Author

Ken Fox was born in Cleveland, Ohio, on July 7, 1924, and moved to Brooklyn when he was about six years old. As a young man he was part of the protests of the hootenanny folk song movement, which embraced Pete Seeger, The Weavers, Arlo Guthrie, and others. He had a lifelong interest in music and was a prolific composer of classical and jazz music on the piano and the electronic clavinova.

Throughout his life he spoke out against injustice, actively protesting the New York State Police attack against Paul Robeson and the persecution and prosecution of Julius and Ethel Rosenberg during the paranoia of the Cold War and the House Un-American Activities Committee. He also spoke out against the Vietnam War and was a draft counselor, supporting the young men who in good conscience could not support our government's unjust war.

When he left his first marriage and moved to Berkeley, California, in 1960, his FBI dossier followed him. He was unable to find work until he was given political refuge on the San Francisco waterfront as a ship's clerk. A sensitive and thoughtful man, he had difficulty fitting in with the macho environment of the waterfront. When he began to write poetry and essays about life on the waterfront to counter the boredom of ship's clerk work, he found his niche. In 1979, seventeen of his poems appeared in *The Waterfront Writers: the Literature of Work*, published by Harper and Row.

Ken's creativity did not stop at music and writing. He was also a fabulous cook and had the curiosity of a free child, becoming interested in meditation and hypnosis along the way. After years of training in hypnosis he became a Certified Clinical Hypnotherapist and left the waterfront in 1981. He developed a well-known practice working with musicians and other performing artists, writers, and pregnant women. For many years he lectured on the subject of hypnosis at most music departments in the Bay Area. For two years he conducted a hypnosis practicum for birth educators. He worked up until a year before his death in 2001, when he became too ill to continue.

Ken left behind his wife, Rose, of 41 years, his daughter, Lisa, and son, Bill, who died a year after his father, his stepdaughter, Andrea, and grandsons Roland and Kurt.

Contents

Eyelight

Ode to a Raindrop

I stared at a raindrop,
Wondering how my eyelight got inside.
I stared at a raindrop,
Wondering if this bit of moisture
Was on a Japanese rosebush
Three weeks before.
Then picked up by the warm winds
Of the east-bound current,
It traveled across the sea
And it landed on my window
In front of me!

I opened the window slowly,
So as not to disturb
This small, dazzling bit
Of nature's splendor.
Sunlight placed a radiant star
Within this tiny globe,
And I was enchanted by the thought;
Someone in Japan
felt the same as I
when their eyelight
got inside!!

—Ken Fox 1/13/78

2

On the Way to Hawaii

> I deign to
> say
> I'm in a plane
> flying
> the ocean main?
>
> It occurred
> to me
> to be
> specific.
> It is
> the calm
> Pacific!

An Eclipse

I heard (saw) a sky full of thunder
Turn into a single
Drop of
Rain
When the Earth passed between
Man's Mind and the
Sun

Fog

Foggy fog
Misty Swirls of Grey
Soft Velvet images
Fade in and out of
Light play intermingles
With spiral wisps of Misty
Dewy dampness glistens
On Leaves Sparkling
Diadems make precious
Tiaras out of webs
Sunrays penetrate
Caressingly
Lifting gently gray
Ribbons of blue
Horizons appear.
Day unfolds in the Blush
Of a Dying fog.

Hummingbird

Heisty Feisty Hummingbird
Twitting on a Twiny
Branch.

Twittery, flittery Hummingbird
Dizzily, busily, fleetely
Hither and yon.

Seeking, Peeking with
Long needle Like Beaking
Within Ambrosiatic
Flora.

Then on Fleeting, winging
Returning to its twiny
Branch to Twittle
Once againing.

Untitled

I watched a milkweed seed
　Pillowed on a gentled breeze
　　Float by my window.
　　　It curtsied twice
　　　　Pirouhetted once
　　　　　And off it went
　　　　　　In a flurry.

Short Scene By Me

In a brilliant splash of
Star spun light
The fabric of a rippled
Stream
Pours forth in shimmering
Beauty
Luxuriantly dappled
With a smattering of Moon beams
The shore appears in a silhouette of
Fluorescent waves and the
Shadowy shapes of trees seem to float upon

The surface of the
Stream
Human eyes compellingly attracted by the
Sheer beauty of the
Scene
PIERCE
The brain and the pupils dilate
to take in more of the
Splendor!
Diadems of light cast off the stream
Play an everchanging
Constant
    Moving
        Thought-upon the brain…

The beholder is at once gentled by the sight and
Soothed by the sound of the
Lapping waters and the mild rasp of the
Cricket accented by the
Mellow bellow of a
Bull frog
Completes the images
Seen by the mind of
ME!

Concert Artist

I think of what it must
  Be like to lift a Bow
   and upon
     One Stroke
      Change
       the
Plastic Placid
  Concrete Block
    Artificial-leather-lined,
      Mink-Coated Chair
       First Row
        Center
         Auditorium
          into
           a
Sparkling Dazzling
      Mercurial
        Orb
         of
          Spinning Webs
           And
            Mountain Tops
             of
              Flowing Streams
               And
                of
                 Deep Chrome Chasms
                  Split By
                   Pale
                    Pastel
                     Skies!

War Zone

A Letter from a G.I. to a Vietnamese

I Watched a Child Die –
Her Arms and Legs
Burned to a crisp by Napalm.
Her eyes exuded Pus instead
of Tears.
The Plastic Bow Clip on her head
was Welded to her Scalp
and there was No Hair.

The Odor of Burnt Flesh
came out of her – very – dying – breath –
For she Was Burned Within As Well.
Death was a matter of minutes away.
I waited – wondering how much of what
I felt could be put into words.
Would anyone believe me?
Or would it be – That what I See
Would Have to Remain with Me!

I sat Down – Not too far away –
To Ponder over What I had Seen.
Then I heard what Sounded like
A whimper and there –
A Small Woman crouched
Next to the Child's Body.
A Moan of Horror shook her tiny frame.
The contortions of sorrow forced

Her Arms and Head to move in an
Awful Way.

She Picked the Body Up
And tore her blouse Apart
Then put her warm, Milk-Filled Breast
to the Mouth of this once
Living Being – and Rocked – and Rocked
And Rocked – And Rocked.
What more can I Say?

YOU looked now with my eyes –
for I wonder What you Would Say
If At That POINT
YOU WERE ORDERED TO KILL HER!
I Heard the Words and tried to form my lips to say
"HOW CAN I!"
Instead I said
"Yes Sir!"
Would you believe this?
Would you Understand?
Could you Understand?

HAH***MAN***LISTEN
The Captain Said
KILL HER
"This is a War Zone – No Civilians"
MAN – THIS IS A WAR ZONE
A WAR ZONE
I CAN**KILL LEGALLY**

I felt a profound wave of Sorrow –
Tragic Eyes looked up at me –
Tears Flowing –
The Man Said – "Kill her for your Safety"
"She'll tell the enemy where you are Going –
Kill her for your safety – **Kill Her**
THAT'S AN ORDER!
I LOOKED AT HER AND BEFORE MY EYES SHE
changed into a Bitch with a Dead Pup –
I had to change her into something more
Killable –

I shot the Child in the Head Knowing
She was Already Dead – The woman looked at the
Bullet Hole and then at Me – and with a feeling
of Utter Despair – I put a bullet between Her
Eyes, too – THIS IS A WAR ZONE
I*ME*CAN KILL LEGALLY

They tell me it's Patriotic to Kill –
They tell me it's the right thing to do – TO KILL
They tell me if I don't Kill Them they will KILL ME.
The Hole oozed blood – both bodies fell to the Ground –
The breast dripped a mixture of Dirt
Blood and Milk.

12

CAN ANY GOD**ANY GOD AT ALL**EVER
FORGIVE ME?

None that I know – Sorrow – None
Feeling – None
Who am I?

I write to you – A total Stranger – in the hopes
that you will Hear Me!
**I KILLED YOUR MOTHER – YOUR SISTER –
   SOMEONE
IN YOUR FAMILY**
I KNOW I DID – I KNOW I DID

I am sorry.

Simple Arithmetic
(Compounded by War)

Windsong blows
Through glistening trees.
Each leaf and limb
Dance entranced
As Wind chimes play
A song of evening
Upon a pool of Cambodian blood
Reflecting the sun of the Mekong Delta.

A bird sings a strange song perched on a
Floating headless body of a Viet-Cambodian mother
With child still within.
A G.I. gasps at the sight
And the last thing he sees is her body.
In a short while he too will begin to float
Bloated with the gas of decay
And thus he will join the list of American
Casualties.

The man comes around to count. She is counted as two
And he spins around until he is dizzy and he counts her over
    and
Over and over and over until there are 3,497 dead enemies
    and
One dead G.I did it all.

50,067 dead G.I.s
figure two children for each
And one wife.

150,000 people more or less
a good size town – nothing to sneeze at –
Let's see how many people will mourn them
50,000 wives, 100,000 children
50,000 mothers, 50,000 fathers
100,000 aunts and uncles
50,000 grandparents or 100,000
100,000 nephews and nieces and
100,000 friends or more and
countless people who just knew them.
How many mourn – add it up –
700,000 minimum.

$50,000 to train him – $50,000 just to keep him there.
At least $20,000 (which you and I didn't pay) to raise him
And $1,000 for his funeral, $10, 000 for his insurance.
He cost at least $131,000 to be killed.
The Cambodian woman cost the U.S. $42.97
(Add that to his cost – she was his only civilian victim)
All totaled: $131,042.97
In round figures
$50,000 times $$131,000 = $6,550,000,000.00
That's cheap – real cheap – for the government of the U.S.
But mighty costly for the family.

It takes a long time – 18 to 20 years to raise him and a lot
Of money for a family to lose –
just for the Love of War???
The Love of Country???
Fight Against communism???
Or What???

Generations

Lisa

Troubled child of my troubled heart
How could I leave you?
How could I not?
To turn away
To turn toward me
Would bring us pain
But, don't you see
In so doing,
we would both be free!

I love you Lisa!

An Ode to Billy

(Whom I Left at Age 9)

How do you feel, Billy Boy, Billy Boy?
How do you Feel!!!!
Remember when – remember when you were
    1 2 3 4 5 6 7 8 9
Remember?

Remember when you were 1 2 3?
It must have been at 4 5 6
But I am sure it was at 7 8 9
that I left you.

Remember when at 10 11 12
the world got awfully dark
at 13 14 15
It was almost over at 16 17 18

When then you found me at 18.
And at 18-1/2 I found you.
I hope that some time in the
Future we will find each other.

Generation Gap

Father

Remember '34?
        For What?
Remember those who died?
        Where?
Remember the Gas?
        Why should I?
Remember how we started?
        How come?
Remember the Bayonets?
        Did they use them?
Remember – I was there – I was one of them…
        And what did you accomplish?
Remember – We organized the Unions –
        So – what did you get?
Remember – you don't remember!!
        You were too young to know!!!!

Son

I am not too young to know – I remember '69. Do you?
        For what?
Remember those who died?
        Where?
Remember the Gas?
        Why should I?
Remember the Bayonets?
        Did they use them?

Remember I was there – I was one of them…

               And what did you accomplish?

We tried to make a better world…

               So did we.

You failed.

               So did you.

You failed me.

               You failed me.

We failed each other.

               I can't talk to you when you don't
remember.

I can't talk to you when you don't listen.

— 1969

Reflections of My Father

When I was young
it was difficult
to say hello to my father.
There were many years
I said that to him
in a voice full of emptiness and resentment.
I did not know how much that
simple word would mean to me some day.
It used to be a greeting made
from a place of youthful anger
which remained unabated
till I grew to know and to love him.
Now I wish I could greet him more often.
The chasm of youthful anger
has been replaced by the
middle portion of these United States
and the ongoing phenomenon of time.

So with many years upon us,
and fewer left for him,
now goodbye has become
the difficult word to say.
We are both fully aware of
its meaning and significance.
Maudlin I am not, nor do I intend to be,
As you will see.
It is an awareness of me, to such degree
that I perceive him deeply within.

He is as much a part of me as my heart and brain.
In that sense there are no farewells.
We begin for each other as an endless chain.
Celebrate with me as I show you the man
from whence I came.

I know him in a way he doesn't know.
I know the very essence of his soul.
I can look at him as a man
and a friend,
as well as my father.
It wasn't until I set my children free
that I could see this most clearly.
Freedom is the key to growth and maturity.
It opens the door of choice
and I thank my father for giving it to me.
I also thank my children for accepting
it from me and hope they use it sagaciously.

I realize how profound his genetic sense is
and I see in my children
a reflection of a reflection
which is his.
In my grandchildren,
I see a spectacular image of lineage
and know his being
is mirrored
in all of us.

I love my father dearly,
For the gift of life
He so willingly

Shared with me
and I appreciate the
chance he took
when he raised me.
He knew, then,
Little of what I would be.
Nonetheless his interests
were models for me to see
At first, they appeared more clearly
in my older brothers.
To my chagrin, the best I could do
was to mimic them,
whereas I feel now
they, very much,
are a part of
my being!

As a young man
I never quite understood
the relevance
of his image!
Until one day, recently,
my daughter, Lisa
told me, poignantly,
how vital my music
was to her!
I questioned this
and at first objected, vehemently,
fearing I damaged her unintentionally!
She said ,"Not at all!"
It gave her the seed

for her garden to grow;
much as my father
gave me the seed for mine.
I am extremely grateful to her
for having shared these reflections
With me.

Over the years I have grown
to see my father from an
even loftier perch,
and let me tell you
I enjoy his being more and more.
He has given me the ability to search
with a never-ending curiosity,
to seek life
in all its splendid forms.
He is a painter and a poet
with a deep love for music.
He is a voracious reader and critic.
He could have been more generous
with his praise.
However, he is a perfectionist in his way;
he sees praise does not always pay.
I won't fault him for that.
I can understand well
for I seek the same in my way.
I learned to enjoy all kinds of foods, since
He is a singular gourmet!
He enjoys laughter,
and is a bit of a raconteur.
Unlike me, he is able to cry!

He fought for men and women's rights
in politics, in unions, and in
tenant's councils.
When he was eighty three
he went to see
the Governor of New York
To plead the plight of the aged.
I come by my sense of me,
through him, most directly.

So, if and when, we say
our last farewell,
it will not be without his
knowing the richness
of the legacy he left me!
I am happy he is still around
To read this,
And though I have some trepidations
for what he will say,
I celebrate my love for him
The same way I celebrate my life,
with zest and joy.
After all it was he who gave it to me.

December, 1978

Thoughts Upon My Mother's Death

My Dawn began as a pregnant seed in a peach tree town.
"You'll see, some day I'll be dead!" she said.
On a hot, red, flame-streaked day waiting for
my mother's womb to relax enough for me to settle in.
"You'll see, someday I'll be dead!" she said.

My mother's coffin lay open and her powdered white
undertaker's face belittled her death.

I was born 12:01 AM on the seventh day of the seventh month
of the year nineteen hundred and twenty four in
Cleveland, Ohio.
"You'll see, someday I'll be dead!" she said.
I don't know if there was a moon.
I was a breach birth, and bear the marks of the forceps
on my forehead.

My father rushed to kiss her one more time.
"You'll see, someday I'll be dead!" she said.
His tears stained the whiteness and ran down her cheek
as if she, too, mourned her death.
They closed the lid.

I was five, living in Pittsburgh, Pa.
A cop killed my dog, Nellie, and my mother took him to court
and got him fired from the force.
"You'll see!" she said.

The funeral home was ten stories high, like a hotel.
There were people pointing to my brothers and saying,
"She also has a son who lives in California."
I didn't tell them it was me.

"Someday!" she said.

My hair at age six was covered with bubble gum.
I fell asleep with it in my mouth.
My mother cut my hair off.
Shorn of my locks I cried and cried and cried.
"You'll see someday!" she said.

Not a tear, not one when she died.
Just a dry, parched, pain wracked my throat.
A fierce headache penetrated through my very being
and a feeling of sadness overwhelmed me.
"I'll be dead someday!" she said.

At sixteen I went into the CCC.
She kissed me goodbye.
And at seventeen I went into the Army.
She rode with me to Penn Station.
I was sad and mad and glad she was there.
She kissed me goodbye.
Her youngest was off to war.
All her children – three sons were off to war.
"Someday!"

The closed the door of the hearse.
The coffin's weight was still in my hand.

"Mom!" I would say
"How many times do I have to tell you not to call me at work!"
and "Yes, I'll tell the kids to kiss you hello when they see you!
How's Pop? The job's okay. Mom, I've got to go. The boss is
waiting!
I don't know when we'll see you next
It will be soon.

Yes, I love you. Now, please, I've got to go!"
"Someday I'll be dead!" she said.

The hearse pulled away.
We were lined up so many to a car.
I was in the first car with Pop and my brothers.
We joked about riding in a limousine and
what it was like to have a chauffeur.
"Someday!" she said.

The ride through the city was unreal.
It was a perfect day for a funeral.
A New York winter-fall sun filtered through a cloudy haze
made people, buildings, trees and things ethereal.
"You'll see!" she said.

We fought over the piano – that someday is here.
She fought with my Dad – that someday is here.
She yelled at the kids – that someday is here.

The hole was six feet deep covered with fake, green grass.
A bower was formed by a tree.
She carried me for nine months.
I only had to carry her three minutes.

The life that gave me life
that brought me into being was now gone.
The "someday" that frightened me as a child was here.
The wind blew gently as I said goodbye and it is only now,
many years later, I acknowledge her death and my love for
her.

"You'll see!" so she said and so I did.

— 7/17/78

A Visit to My Brothers

Am I
A sense of we!
A sense of me
being a place in his mind,
as he looked at me across a table
three feet wide,
three thousand miles away.

The day I arrived
We left on a journey
down the track of his time.
Carefully seeking
safe places to be together,
mostly in the past.

We sat together
riding in a strange train
Of disharmony.
Afraid to break
the ties of blood,
to let the tears flow,
to intermingle our thoughts
in the sera of who we are!
And to share in the feeling
of having come through
the same place
at different times,
of having known an earth
with our genetic sense!

Now the time has come
to speak openly and freely
of those things
which we are made of!
And feel, for once,
the magnetic tide,
the pulsating ebb and flow
of a shared energy!
We! Us! My brothers and me,
there are three of us, you see,
who enjoy the same blood.
The rare form of communality
Found in each family.

How close can we be?
Physical proximity is not significant!
Or is it!

We have, somehow, managed to survive
The ravages of time.
Particularly me,
since I am the youngest of the three
and live the farthest away.
Maybe that is why we have not
mutilated the tie
too severely.

We and my I
Traveled back to the
path of departure.
The three of us,
plus the entire family,

said our goodbye with
a sense of beginning and
a sense of againess!

I felt a sense of awareness
that I wanted to live more,
to share the
energy of my brothers,
to see and
to be
three again,
in a room where words give way
to a shared pulse,
to a feeling of love
of my family
that only my father,
my mother, may she rest in peace,
and my brothers
can share with me.

— 10/78

To My Wife's Father – May He Rest in Peace

To wit – A Father I should be!
To Whom – I am not sure.
To my wife – how could I be?
For my sperm could not sire that
which I desire!!

My love of her to bear fruit of mind
or progeny alone for me.
Not willfully do I demean
Nor do I care to be Ghost Reincarnate
Of someone I knew not of.

Nor do I want to be none other than me
so that I may sleep with her and she with me
Without Violation of his Soul!!

Waterfront

Four Thirty to Six pm

Lights stream – Horns Blow –
Screeches Squeal
As People Steal
Rolling Spaces
For Their
Wheels

Up Tempo – Four Thirty
To Five – Intersections
of Motors Roar –
Colored in
Shades of
Exhausted Black and
Blue.

Elevator Cables Whine
as they Untwine
and Escalators Step
Up their Steps.
Office Doors Close
Under Pressure and
The odor of Five to Five
Sweat Permeates
the Scene.

Locks keyed by the Last to
Leave – Alarms Set –
Secured Uniforms begin
To Patrol

As the Mood of the City
Changes.

People flow into corridors
of Homeward Direction –
Forming Impatient, Hungry,
Bulbous Clumps at Crossings –
Moving in Singular Minds
to points of Departure.

A Billion Dollars Worth of
Massive Transportation
Moves to Chits, Tokens, Paper Coupons
And Depressed Gas Pedals.
Blue Chip Stamps are
Dialed into the Glove Compartments of
The Gasless Commuters.
As Those That Missed the Pump
Sit Bravely in a Sea of
Motored Anger.

Five Forty Five to Six.
A Million Doors Open
and shut and Four
Million Men
Women and
Children
Say
Hello
to Each
Other.

Slow Time in the Hiring Hall!

Talk – Talk a wide mouth, square toothed, jut jaw
Moves up and around a tight-lipped smirk,
While a slack-jaw smile listens to the jive.

Bare light-bulb thoughts
make the bench even harder to sit on
and the "Jive" is nothing but "Two Word Down,"
No "Ups" when the work is slow!

Listen to "Fat Lips: con the game
with a slap of the deck and "Who's dealing?"
The table's quiet, save for the rustling of an old paper
with the ink read off of it. Nobody takes the challenge!!

Headline talk is done. Lips turn down and one by one,
like a chant, they cry "No Work!!"
Twiddled thumbs and tapping fingers mingle with twitched
        eyelids,
scuffed chairs and shuffled shoes
and the boredom sinks in LIKE THUNDER!!

"What's Happening, Man?"

Talk – Talk! "Two days last week – three the week before –
None this week – maybe there ain't no more!!
"Wide Mouth" smiles "What you complaining about, Buddy?
With all the money you got – you best go home and lock
        the door!!"
"Tight Lips" smirks "Look who's talking – with a big Cad
        and a

sweet woman, who better lock whose door??" and "Slack
        Jaw's" smile
turned into a droop with half-lidded eyes – nothing there,
        man.
Not even a nod. The body's here but a sick sleep from
        waiting has
taken hold and the boredom sinks in ever deeper and more!!

The dispatch window opens and a sense of fear and
        expectation
goes flying round the room. Muscles twitch in pain and addled
brains send messages to fifty sets of ears to listen for their
numbers. The grey haired, smiling face of the dispatch man
looks out into the hall and he calls – one number, two, three
then four. "Man, it's going to hurt if he has to call some more.
I don't want to work no how!!" The next is five then six –
pick up sticks – and when seven is called the man with the
        deck
slaps the cards down and hollers
"Why me? Ain't we supposed to be free?"

The rest of the bodies relax. The shuffled, scuffled, scuffing
        of shoes,
newspapers and chairs signal a return to the mindlessness and
the boredom sinks even further in!!
"Hellos" go to a few more brothers and "Old Talk" is renewed.
The dispatch man says "No more today!!" and like a shot
        out of nowhere -
doors open – feet fly, and faces smile.
"Maybe no pay but I sure as hell got the day and
that ain't no lie!!
See you tomorrow, good buddy!!"

Clerk's Shack

Sitting in a barren brain box
Built with two by fours
A lighted Light Bulb
Casts its ugly rays
upon
Eclipsed Eyes
that see
Nothing
to
hear
Nothing
to
Say.
Except sit upon
a pedestal
of Fatty
Flesh
and think Nothing
to do.
Nothing
except Sit
in a Barren Brain Box.
Limbo for a
Day's
Wage.

To The Insombulant

In the wee small hours of the briny night –
the flea-bitten hound wails on a mighty mite –
The sound of the moon makes the rafters quake
and the egg-bound chickens give a mighty shake –
The crestfallen heroes of bygone wars
sing the praises of the whores of yore –
and I, me hearty, toss and turn
    in a sleepless pit
        unfit for the dead
            or the living!!

— Pier 48B
6/13/74

Structural Steel

God! Man – they turned on the World
Eight AM – the sun shines bright
a million skillion starter buttons
receive the Finger….
Zm Phow afuttatuttafuttatuttafuttatta
Compressed Air Hoses gorge themselves
full of VDRRRAP
and MAN
grabs his vibrating
ball of a building
Crusher – as a
Girder arises
on the slender
wire of a
Craning Neck of the
Foreman's Whistle –

Shrieking
Up there – Down is a button
on a Lift Load of Lumbering
Caterpillars pushing up a
Side of a Mountainous Pile
of Nails Hammered
into a Tongue and Groove
Floored by the sound of a
Rivet Gun peening in a Hollow
Wall – Oh!! But for the blast
of a Lunch Whistle – fingered

buttons stop –
Afuttafuttatufutta-fu-ta-fu-ta

Compressed Air Hoses sag
Lunch is in the bag – no Gag
Come One O'Clock we're going
To do some more.
Asleep astraddle girders
Ten stories up – Sun High
Somebody Bangs!!!

God! Not again – Gasoline
Tanks full of Shimmering
Heated Bodies Rise
Aztufastrak-zap a torch
to the Steel Button
and a million skillion
pistons pass a fart-reaching sound
of futtattafuttatafuttatafuttattafuttatut
to start the afternoon.

Hey! Bang – Bang
We lost our angle
and the Tempo
of the foreman's Pulse beats
Rivers of sweat
Into stories of How
The Wild West was Won
Laying Iron
Rails on the side of the
Golden Gate Bridge

So you can walk across
The Continental Shelf
Without Falling.

Hey! Up There! Down here is
the foundation – Twelve wheeled
Trucks with Rolling Cones
Unlatch the Hatch and
Out the Spout
Concrete evidence of man's abililty to
Expand His waistline on the backs of
Labor-Saving Devices to make
Man pour concrete into
His Form – Reinforced
By Rods up his –

As for his understanding of world and man
He has none
He is being paid for Eight
That's all he cares about – No Shit
Man – Eat – Sleep and
Be To Work On Time – Drive
A Caddy '59

Hey! Up There! Over Here!
Watch it now! Watch it Now!
Hey Man – move a hair
This thing might slip and
Then where!! Hold that guide –
Gotta make Five – Heavy date
Easy Now! The day is done –
See you – Sun – Tomorrow.

Three pm coffee at Carmen's Dock
Restaurant

Sounds of a Coffee Break bounce off
a refrigerator door.
A bottle of beer slides down a
sleek formica bar making
Shhhh
As a cup collides with a saucer
Making a
Gadonk.

Voices mingle with the nervous
squeal of stool tops – and the
density of conversational smoke
rises and falls with the intensity
of the sound.

More people arrive –
The sharp song-like voice of the
Phillipine Waitress cuts, knife like,
through the dull muddle of male inanity.
If cattle could Cackle as well as Low
Your ear could clearly hear the scene.

Chairs, pushed by momentary owners,
sound off in angry rasps – resenting the
inertial pause – and vent inanimate anger
by tripping Man as he Departs.

No more Coffee – coffee over –
Heads nod – days end is near.

Empty bottles make melodic sounds as
they are put away and the soft sound of the
wiping rag Hushes the Coffee Urn.
The register Jangles "No Sale."

The door is Locked and given a
final security shake.
The inanimate objects left inside
now become animate only from what is
left of the outside rumble of the Day.
"See you, Man – in the morning."

80 C

80 C is a letter and a
number to you – to me
It's a job – It's people –
It's a whole world of
Trucks and ships, and
Silks and Satins, Cashews
And Boredom, Coffee and
Hernias, Cotton and Death
   And Just Plain People
      Who talk about
Silks and Satins, Horses
And Boredom, Ball Games and
Hernias, and
   Who Died over the Weekend!!
That's Eighty Cee, See!!

Pier 26–Longshore Lunch Room

It's a dark Dank Day
For sitting in a Five Table Room
With Ten Long Benches
That no one else is sitting on.

It's Abysmally Dismal.
Graffittied walls
Speckled with Crushed Bugs,
Spittle and Beer.
Table Tops covered with
Thick Layers of
Decayed Lunch.

One Light,
too bright to look at,
too Dark to read by.
No Windows!
No Nothing!
The Lone Radiator
Heats itself and
Nothing else.
Darkened corners of uncollected
Garbage give off
Foul Odors of Past
Activity.

I sit waiting for the
Next Job and try –
Desperately – to Daydream
Myself out of existence.

Tour Guide

Written in commemoration of the real Pier 39

History shows,
not long ago,
great ships
Used to dock here!
What we are standing on
was once called a finger pier!

When they shut the docks down
San Francisco became a carnival town!
Now the only place you can see what a
longshoreman looked like
is in the wax museum!

They have an exhibit of freight
at the restaurant called "Pier Thirty Eight!"
And for your further edification
they have a show called "Immigration"
at the "Pier of All Nations."

Now! I want you all to look around.
For you are standing on hallowed ground!
It was here in Nineteen Thirty Four
that the great longshore union was born!
And there's a model of their hiring hall
down on the mall!

There is lots more to see!
So don't go 'way!
The Belly Dancers are free!
Have a nice day
in the city Herb Caen calls
"Baghdad by the Bay!"

— October 1978

48

Shop Talk

Sitting in a battered brain box,
   Hearing searing sound.
      Gutteral
                  convoluted
                        syllables

Words of empty brains
Scattered on the winds.
   Made by hissing throats –
      ejected from
         compressed
            molded
               squarely
                  folded
                     minds.

Flabby lips and thickened tongues
   from insipid inanities.
      each mind prances around
         the sound
            trying to comprehend
               the meaning
                  of
   Vehicular – Ejaculating
               Home-Run
            Lamborghinni!
   Cinematic fruit on
Twelve Orgiastic Cylinders

Emission Control
  Sits Heavy –
    Heavy
      on
      my
      mind!!

Eight Solid Concretely Impervious Hours
  of impacted wisdom toothless
    Thought
Just to make a buck – my head
    Screams
      In
    Tortured Disbelief
     that such
       cunning
        a
       contrivance
      as a
    dolorous dollar bill
could hold and hold and fold
    these addled minds –
     including mine.

What, pray, can this mantle be
  that enshrouds and encapsulates
  my soul and demeans
    us all
to say Nothing to Each Other –
  Our Talk "man to man"

Does not hold
  a single
    sound
      of
      Love
A syllable of Compassion
  An utterance of Peace –
    To say the least.

Say no more – for – fretful
  they shall be – fearful
    that these words
      will change
        their
          mold!
They will scream
          In
Contorted rhetoric
"MOTHER FUCKER
    MASSERATI
      VW
        STICK SHIFT
          FIVE ON THE FLOOR
            UP YOURS!"

      and
I understand
  every
  word

they
say
and
that
is
S A D!!

Brother – all I want to say
   is PEACE
    and
    only
  the buck
Will make you understand.
"Buddy can you spare a dime!!"

— *December 2, 1975*
Pier 80A

Warm Beings

John Green—the Owner of the Face
on the Barroom Floor

John Green is a wild old man – a wild old man is he –
He called for his friends – he called for his wife
and his children to fiddle-dee-dee
    and around the shadow of death
      he danced!!!!

With a bottle of booze in one hand – and his eyes riveted
    On the cross –
John Green said, aloud, for the world to hear "Don 't mourn
my soul – I never done harm to no one
    but St. Pete's gonna send me to Hell
      for not never usin' my skull!!

John Green looked at me one day and said "I don't drink
    for pleasure – I drink to live." And I heard the angels
cry for his soul, for no mortal man has to suffer the way
    John Green has!!!!

Bottled up in his skull are thoughts that no man has thought,
and sights through his eyes that no man has seen, and sounds
that no man has heard and when John Green goes, so goest
    they
      and we of the living will be just a little
        poorer and Satan will gain his riches!!!!

JOHN – JOHN – dya hear me JOHN? Dya hear for what
    I have
to say? I want you to know it's the truth!!!! Before you die,
John – John Green, I want to know what's inside your skull. I

want to know how a man like you has suffered. Then,
        John Green,
when you tell me all, then, old man, you can die, but not until
then, John Green, will I let you rest. Not until then,
        John Green!!!!

You have no right, John Green, to go to hell!!!! You have
        no right,
because the hell on earth that you have seen is enough
        for four
score or more, and I make my plea to old Saint Pete – let my
friend, John Green, enter the pearly gates. He ain't done
wrong
        to no one!!! He ain't done wrong to no one!!!
St. Pete, listen to me now. John Green brought up his kids –
took care of each and every one!! Made sure to thank the Lord
each morning, noon and night!!! Lord, Lord, you and St. Pete
have got to save his soul!!! Why, he bought round after round
at Riordan and nary a word to no one that it was he,
        John Green,
that refreshed their mortal souls. Now, Lord, a man like that
can't be all bad, can he!!!

St. Pete, you gotta hear. John Green dasn't owe nary a cent
to no one!!! John Green is a man of his word!!! Ain't too
many
men around this earth you can trust any more and
        John Green is
one!!! Hear me! Hear me, St. Pete, and you, dear Lord.
Hear me!
        Don't send my friend, John Green, to Hell.
                He ain't done wrong.

As these words I spoke I suddenly saw the most ominous
	sight
		and heard the most ominous sound – and thought
		the most
			ominous thought!!!!

"John Green – John Green" I heard the Lord say. And
	I looked
around and saw Him there. And his words rolled like thunder
	and his eyes flashed with fire.
"John Green, your friends have made the greatest plea that I
	have ever heard!!!
I'll let you enter Heaven if you tell them all you know,
and if you don't, John Green, then to Hell for ever more
	You'll go!!!!"

"John Green – John Green, I, the Lord, hath spoken. Tell
	all you
know of life, and death will be a peace for you. Tell all
about the mines – and the winter nights – and the work you
worked and the soul you almost sold – almost sold to the
Devil and fought like a man to keep it. Tell all, John Green,
and I, the Lord, will let you through the gates to live
	In heavenly peace.

"What's that you say, John Green? What's that that I hear?
You say you need a bottle of booze to do it, man!!!!. Is that
what I hear you say?!! Why, how can a man like you destroy
your mortal soul any more than you have already done so?
How, John Green? How?!!!"

Then John Green answered Him. He said "Thanks, Lord,
	for each

day and each night. I know you weren't a drinkin' man and
I know I done wrong with my skull, but my Heaven is my
        bottle
and my hell is without it. I drink to keep alive, my Lord.
        I drink
to keep alive!!!! And thanks, my friends, for pleading, but
        my story
is too sad for you to hear and I'm saving it for Satan, for – "
and at this point John Green rose up and lifted his right
hand skyward. "When Satan hears my story, Hell will
        freeze over
and Heaven will return to Earth and the mortals will be
        returned
                to Eden.!!!!"

Thus, when the Devil heard this he made arrangements to
        keep
John out. And the Lord wouldn't let him in. And now I know
why John Green drinks to stay alive. Now I know, for if he
        drinks
long enough, the Devil has got to let him in and then Eden
will return to Earth, and John Green will die in a Heaven he
has created for everyone else but John Green –

To Kathy — Chrysalis

A Woman to a child
>   Is a Mother
>   A Mother to a Child
>   Is a Woman.

A Woman-Child is
>   Neither
>   Child
>   Nor Woman.

A Woman-Child
>   That is a Mother
>   Is a Child.

A Child that is a Child
>   With a Mother
That is a Mother
>   Will be a
>   Woman!

To Rudy – A Black Ex Con

I know a man who did twelve years for being hooked!
This man's face has got a moan for a look!
He plays a Horn Forlorn, A Riffless Riff – a combination
wail and a Hymn.

He's been so low – so long – to him the Up he knows
does not belong in the world of man for his Ups are
lower than the lowest lows!

He plays in muted tones – a song so sad that mortal
fear is struck in those of us that choose to hear
what he has to play!!

If humanity could do this to him – then I wonder if we
who are supposedly free would rather not choose to die
than live in his kind of agony!

I cry, freely, in his presence. There is nothing I can say.
I feel sorry more for me – for the reflection that I see,
in some unbelieving way, could actually be me!

Then when I see my eye in his I say goodbye and,
cowardly,
I hope never to meet him again until I die!!!!

The Bass Player

To my friend, Warm John, the Bass Player

He slapped my hand
the same way he slapped a string;
in an all knowing, soft and gentle way!
I could feel myself vibrate to his soul.
Then he gave me his love
in the same way
he played a riff.

He was a
down – round man
who could bounce a note
right from the belly of the bass
and make it come across
the bridge
singing Hallelujah like it was the Lord
or singing peace like it was your brother or sister
or singing love like it was your lover.

His sound strutted to the
tune of your head and followed it around
making all kinds of noise!
Never, never would he ever disturb your peace.
He was a bass man's bass man
who entered through a door
for which he needed
no key!

He can bend a sound
to fit around your heart
and make you feel it is your art,
not his, that made you
play that way!

He plucked a note
from my book and made it "Blue."
Then, with sleight of hand he made it "Red" and,
with a flick of his wrist,
he made it go round and round
inside my head!

He "is" when he "isn't!"
There are no words to say.
You'll know what I mean
the next time you hear him play.
let him lay five on you the way he layed them on me
and you'll see an extraordinarily,
beautiful human being!

—10/78

A Seeker

Museums of My Mind

I. The Heritage Gallery

This is a room of origin,
of old empty canvasses of unseen ancestors.
of a collage of my mother's eye, my father's nose, my
    grandfather's cheekbone
cemented on an ovum,
painted in faded baby blue.
There is a genealogical tree of copulation
showing all of my relations.
Sculpted in basrelief is the influenza germ
that killed my maternal grandparents.
The tapestry on the far wall shows the
route my father took when
he fled the religious persecution of his native land.
There are three bronze hands – the gnarled one holding the
jewelers loupe is my grandfather's. He was a
watchmaker. The second, a delicate one, indeed,
 belonged to my mother. She was
a pianist. The third, poised on a stone etching of an American
Indian is my father's. He is a lithographer.
If you wish to have sound during your visit,
press the button,. You will hear my grandmother's
screams at birth. Caruso singing O Sole Mio.
Songs of Russia, Germany, England
and the American Civil War. You will hear angry cries,
laughter and sobbing of my immigrants. This
room is not recommended for the
depressed or the nostalgic.

II. The Gallery of Youth

The gallery of my youth is thickly carpeted
in an abstract weave of pain and frustration.
Its walls are painted in muted tones
of loss and despair.
Twenty canvasses of pale thought, two murals of experience,
a fountain of tears and adolescent secretions make up the
catalogue for this room.
If you wish to have sound during your visit,
Press the button. You will hear simulated birth screams,
sobs, uncontrolled hysteria and a fourteen year old
sucking his thumb.

III. The Gallery of the Absurd

Enter at your own risk!
Pterydactyls and pirrhana
await your presence.
First, you will be stripped to the bone.
Then you will be allowed to enter my home.
The floor is covered with the concrete impressions
Of every step I have taken!
Be careful. A fall
will be appalling to your mind
and most upsetting to your spine!
The far wall is a collage of my adolescent war in bloody
        cotton candy
and shrapnel made of popcorn. Phallic guns ejaculate
        epithets of fear
and virgin vaginal mouths laugh hysterically as each
        utterance

lays spent at the entrance of the vaunted vault!
Be aware!! Be aware!
The middle of the room is a huge intaglio of my life from
    birth to 35.
It is filled with a slippery slimy substance of doom
    and gloom.
Don't stare at this too long, you may be trapped in my
    miasma of vacillation.
Even worse, you might be caught
in inertia staring at a vacant eye (I).
The only exit from this space
is through a metaphor
that is an apparition of a door.
If you accept the fact you are simply mortal,
it will be much easier to find this portal.
And don't forget to chortle as you leave this place,
lest you take it seriously
and you become a study of me.
I wouldn't mind that in the least.
It would add to my collection,
But what would it do to you, you see!

My House

I live alone.
In a dwelling of my mind.
Distant from reality –
Yet so close that my machinations
Seem to me – real.
The house I live in
Has walls and no walls.
Windowed spaces fit within
Windowless frames and
Doors exist only as
Thresholds – the open
One negated by the closed.

I sit, looking out, and see
the reflection of me looking in
and wonder which is really me.
I am alone no matter which
way it may be.

I walk through the endless
forests within my house.
Some days with dread fear.
I never seem to stop – asleep
or awake – it makes no difference.
My reality is as much a dream
as it is a reality.

Sometimes I hear my own breath
and feel it is another's. Then

there are times when the sound
of my footsteps will make me shudder.
For in my loneliness I am aware
that others do exist.

I live alone
locked in by my thoughts.
Some days my house is full
and I feel real. Those days
are all too few. Most days
my house is barren. The only
comforts then are those that
I will allow. For you see –
I live alone – within me.

— Kenneth J. Fox 10/2/71

Awareness

I'm aware of who I am
When you're aware of me
    And this is
        Wrong!!!

For it should be –

I'm aware of who I AM
When I am aware of
        ME!!!

Thoughts Added to the Rest of Them

What is the EEry Mirror
that is so terse
that it makes the reverse
appear to be true!! (the mind)

The Reflections of a deflection can be a deception!

Pondering is sometimes akin to Wondering
If done over too long a period of time!

Welfare is not Fair for the Poor or the Well!

The Spirit of the Law, particularly now, is nothing
more than that!

The Constitutional Amendments – known as the Bill of
    Rights –
should be amended to hold the Judges in Contempt who
    abuse them.

The Answered Question

What kind of song do you sing
to the Child of your mind?
I should say "I" – for it is I
who is seeking the words and the tune.

Fantacize – What child do you see?
Is it calm? Is it peaceful
Where this child sits, or is it
Violent and unfulfilled?

I don't know why I ask you –
When it is I who is seeking
His whereabouts.

Is the child only a dream – or is
the child someone that you really see?
Does the child stand free or is He bound
by strong ropes of Mind and Matter?

It is my child – I don't know why
I ask you – unless
you see objectively
that which I cannot
or that – which in truth is a
figment of my mind.

In my blindness I look upon you to
reflect my image,
both real and of fantasy –
when it is I who should be

seeing "I" through me –
It is My Song –
It is my Vision
It is My Place
To Find Me!!!

Depression

I wait Day by Day
For Light of some kind.
I wait in a deep grey mist –
For Something – I'm not sure
What!!!

I wait – the characters pass –
Faceless – voices float by –
Devoid of recognizable patterns.
The Mist Writhes about my body and
I am encased in a slowly whirling
Vortex of Nothingness.

I Wait in elasticized time –
Hours – snap in and out of minutes –
Days ferment and the odor of wasted
Time Sickens me.

I Wait – the Mist is fetid and Humid.
The Sweat of a prickled anxiety
Falls in little rills all over Me.

I wait – in Awe of my mind –
Breached in an Agony of
Thoughts encrusted in
Scabby Inertia.

I Wait – For Something –
I Wait – Silence Shatters
The Veil into Myriad
Splinters of Thought.

I reach up – blinded by
The mirror of my Mind –
Groping and Grasping in
Desperation – Trying to cling
To One Idea!!

I Stand Paralyzed –
As the
Last Thought
Passes By.

— Ken Fox, 1978

Just Me

My head is full of meditation
　　　Today.
My self is full of
　　　Me.
I have no strength for the
　　　Outer World.
And want to be – Just to Be.

My thoughts flake off
　　　When they are too heavy
And make deep crevices
　　　Of Rest.

I guess if I can't pull my
　　　Head together
I'll just have to be
　　　Satisfied
Like it or not –
　　　Just to be Me.

For Me

My Mind is like some hair-triggered pistol – ready to
fire –
To discharge – to push out – to expel my thought.
To describe a moment of beauty – for me – I – My –
 eyes to reflect upon
What I see – to disgorge these thoughts of me for
others to
Sometimes See.
Nay, Nay, for me – I'm selfish – if I make a cloud in
words
Or describe my infinite passion – it is for me.

If I sleep with a woman and I describe my intensity –
 it is for me.

If I soar in skies so high, and trees so beautiful –
 it is for me.

It is my pain of awareness – it is my agony – my
ecstasy –
That produced this beauty and if I am willing to
share it
With you – Then by my balls – read it – or tell me
that you
don't want to – but don't read what I have to say and
make light of it.

If you want part of me – then, you have to be honest
Otherwise – Fuck Thee.

Day One After Birth

The warm/cold death of my creation
  saturated my body.
My mind unfolded.
Layer after layer of Brain cells
  passed through an energizer
and pictures of all life – creation
and the center of the Universe
Came into my being.

A Millennium of strife and struggle
Ripped through my muscles
  And my nerves created a pain
So great within
  That I let loose a scream of recognition
  So loud that it awakened all of my senses
And at that point in time
     I Became Alive!
 A flood of tidal proportions
Consisting of
  Light
  Sound
  Smell – and
  Awareness
Shook my every cell
And surge upon surge
Of waves of sensing
Passed through me.
My skin became vibrant and glowed

So intensely that I could feel
    Every
    Sperm
Within my testes
Come alive.

And then suddenly I felt the pulse of my blood
  Coursing through my heart
Setting up a rhythm for each experience
  And implanted the many beats
Permanently within me.

I am now an endless chain of now
  An embodiment of
    What was
    What is
        And
What will be.
  I Am Me!!

Understanding

When will you understand?
That when you don't say
What you mean to say,
You say that which is
Wrong!!

When will you understand?
That meaning must be clear –
Don't Say "Don't Lay"
When you mean
Fuck You!!

When will you understand?
When will you understand
That it is painful
to hear you say
"I Love You"
When if you know not
What you mean,
Then how can you mean
That?!!

When will you understand?
When will you understand
That you can say What you mean
And mean it!!
And I Will Understand
And so Will You!!

Creative Ego

If I am fated never to know
What an Audience is –
Then I must learn
to be Humble.

So that what I Create
Will Ring of Me
And Not some Narcissistic
Fool Involved
In Perfidy!!

If then the Chance
That someone feels as Intense
As I about My Work –
Then I must not humiliate them –
Nor Demean Myself –
By Making Light of it!!!!

If, Lastly, My Work
Should be such to gain
Some Lasting Fame,
Then My Humility
Will Stand Me in
Good Stead, For My Audience
Appreciation will
Be Based upon the

Real Me
And not just My Head!!!

The Corporate Image

I'm Fat and Corpuscular
Obese – and not Muscular.
    Gluttony
Made my Fatty Acids
    Break Down.
And my cellular structure
    Give in!

I'm wide and I'm corpulent –
My affluence creates an Effluvience.
Watch Out – Be Careful
For I could make
A Pollutient
All over You!!!

Upside – Downside Up

I 'm on the downside of an Up
I'm Upside Down –
I feel like a Turtle without a Shell –
A Bear without a Lair
A Hopper without His Grass.

The Upside looks So Good –
That the Downside can't be That Bad!
I feel myself sliding and I remember Now
That I put a Pillow at the Bottom
The Last Time I was there.
It won't be as bad this time
But it Ain't Good.

I Feel Like a Bad Set of Brakes
And there's a Roaring in My Head –
The Air Crackles with all Kinds of
Untranslated Anger –
No Real Place to Rest My Head.
I'm Real Weary – Shot My Load on the
Upside and Now I'm down.

Got to find a stick to put my back on Straight.
Got to find a new set of shoulders to put
My Head On.
Maybe this is the Time to Diet.
A fast or Two might flush my brain

And Lighten the Load and on the
Upside I'll be going!!

Patience Man!!
Keep on Pulling!!]
The Stones Fall Out
And Fertile Soil Remains.
I've got all sorts of New Plants
For this Garden.
So Down is Down
But UP ain't That Far
Away!!

I'm Fifty-Three

I'm fifty three
It takes time
Don't you see!

I'm fifty three
It takes patience
Don't you see!

I'm fifty three
It's not that I don't feel free
Don't you see!

I'm fifty three
It's like things begin to close in
Don't you see!

I'm fifty three
It's only that I want –
just once, to feel me
Don't you see!

Fifty three's not so old
But it is past fifty –
time and patience
run out pretty quick now
Don't you see or
Don't you see!

In Praise of My Nose

A moment,
  God knows,
In praise of
  my nose!!
It's red-ringed
  nostrils and
Bright pink, bulbous
  tip.
Its crystal-clear mucous
  dripping on my lip!!
Its bitter irritations
  and strange electric pains
and penchant for medications
  with unusual names!

A moment, please,
  for the pollens
and all else
  that make me sneeze!!
I might add, once in a while,
  they even make me wheeze!
And Oh! Oh! What an ode I could write
  For the "Cobe in the Nobe!"
Or the snaffle of sniffle you get
  When you whiffle a bit of weed.
    Indeed!!

A moment in praise of my
  Extraordinary snorts,

and stentorian snores
  and those monumental sneezes
    whose spasms send me tumbling
      out of the treeses!!
To the twitches and tics and
  tweaks to my beak.
To my nostrils' red flare which would
  make any decent dragon glare.

Last and by no means least
  A moment of adoration and appreciation
for having been blessed with such a noble appendage
  A veritable organ of smell to wit.
An instrument of stately width and breadth
  of sensuous, rapturous pleasures
and all kinds of hell.
  A moment for the very air it lends to my demeanor.
And, by all means, to the very air it lets me breathe.
  Finally, let trumpets blare in great fanfare!
For without this mighty nose – it goes without saying,
  There is little need for this bit of (sneeze) prose!

My Love To Rose

Dining Out Without You

Flickered
Candle.
Lonely
Teeth.
Chew
Lonely
Food.
Lonely
Taste.
Eaten in
Haste.
What a
Waste!!

My Wife – My Woman – My Rose

A woman's got a body
  with a permanent smile –
and my woman can make it laugh.
When my woman wants to make me feel
  real big
she takes her shoes off
  and stands
underneath my chin
  looking up at me!
My woman's not afraid of wanting it
  or giving it, either
and "it" ain't just sex
it's everything.
My woman's love is
  as peaceful and beautiful
as the earth.
And like nature, she is
  unpredictable
making her love more meaningful to me.
My woman never lets me down.
Her buoyancy keeps
  me afloat.
Lastly – there isn't any –
For this baby is mine.
She knows it and I know it.

(For my dear, lovely Rose – Ken)

To My Rose

Words that I never said to you before!

You asked me to say words - sentences - syntax that
I never said to you before.

The only words that come to mind
are the words of unspoken anger
or the words that do not exist of
unspoken feelings.

The words of anger are words that are no longer a
part of my vocabulary. I could conjure them up
as an exercise - but that is all.

The words of unspoken feelings are not there
because they are buried deeply within me -
within my soul and they are
expressed
in glances - in touch - and warmth - and love - and
physical beingness.

There are also the words of each new day which
really have not been spoken before. They
are the words of love and of thankfulness
and gratefulness that we are
who we are!

There are also the words of Yiddish that have never
been said in the ways that they are being said
today...because they couldn't have been
said because I didn't know them.

Finally, there are the words of a sadness that is
        both known and unknown, spoken and unspoken,
            hopefully we will not be using these
                words for many years to come.
                    Just to know that they
                        are there is enough
                            for now.

— (Signed)
Ken Fox, 12/96

To My Wife – Opus III

Symbiosis

A Somber Pall – a fear of death,.
A Fear of fear that we will not be.

Together we must overcome
what fear you have.

I must see the fear I have as mine
or yours will come alive within me.

Unless we each separate our fears –
I fear that each will see the fear
He or She
Shouldn't See!!

To My wife – Opus V

When Down deep within my soul
I find a path for you and I
to walk on –
Then give me your hand and I will
lead you through my mind,
and show you
the many splendors
I behold!!

Then, with me you will
See and Hear
and Feel and Touch and Taste
My World – and thus
my world will not be mine
Alone!!

With you within me –
my world will be Free!
For then our thoughts can
intermingle! And if you will then
do the same for Me
and lead me through your mind –
then what we share
will be a sense of Total We.

Each word, no longer couched in
veiled thought, will be open.
Needs expressed in a way such as this,
cannot help but be met by Honest
Appraisal and a real attempt to
resolve them.

My Love is coined from the beauty
of your soul and fed from the many
facets of your mind. Enhanced to a point of
ecstacy, so high, that I feel you and I
have merged.

We have sipped of each other's passion.
It is like an ambrosia, so delicate,
that no other mortals on earth can ever
taste of it.

If these be only words and nothing more
then shut these pages from your mind.
But if these words ring with shimmering Truth,
then say aloud – in gentled tone "I love you –
I love you – I love you."
For in this way I will know that you are mine –
and I can rest for I am
already yours.

An Ode to my Beloved Rose On Her Seventy-Fifth Birthday!!

Dearest One,
I have known you, lo, these many magnificent years
and I know, deep within my heart and soul,
That I will know and be with you till the end of time.

You give of yourself freely to me. You give me
your true essence, your spirit and your soul.
I feel your very being pulses within my heart.
Our hearts and souls beat as one.

No matter how much time we have to be together
In this life,
In this body,
Each moment with you becomes more precious than the
one before.
My love and my passion for you, dearest, knows no
bounds.
My words cannot describe the feelings and the pure joy
that you give to me and to my life.
You are my beloved and I cherish all that is you

Happy Birthday Dear!!
I will be with you body and soul
Forever!!
Peace and Love

Ken

To My Dearest Rose
On this Amazing Day
Your Birthday!!!

Birthdays are amazing days.
It is a day that started to be your very special day
even before you were aware that it was your
Birthday. That is how special this day is!!

It is a very special day to me because if that day
did not exist when it did,
then I would never have known you,
and my love would never have been fulfilled
because there could never have been another you!!

My love for you, o'er these many years, my dearest one,
has risen to heights beyond belief. My words can
barely express the feelings I have for you. You are so
precious and dear to me. Your sweet, wonderful love
for me makes me cherish each moment I am with you.
You are my beloved.

Happy Birthday Dear!!! It is a joy to celebrate this day
with you!!! Thank you for being you!!! Each day is a
gift to me and to you and to both of us!!! Thank you
again, dear one!!!

93

To My Rose

The older she gets, the wilder and more stunning
she becomes.
I am awe struck by her beauty and her brains.
I unabashedly adore her
and love her with all my heart
and with every cell of my body.

To this day it is hard for me to believe
that I won her heart and soul
and that I have managed to keep her
through thick and thin
and now, after these many years,
our hearts beat as one.

A Love Poem for My Rose

I have been sitting here
  With not a word to say.
    Nothing seems to come.
      I sit here waiting for the magic
        Synthesis of mind, heart and soul
          To bring forth the words
            To tell you how I feel about you,
              To tell you how much you mean to me.

What I want to say I have
  Written many times before.
    I have said it in poems.
      I have said it in music.
        I have said it with touch.
          I have said it with just a look.
            I have said it in as many ways
              Beyond sounds and sight and touch.
                I have said it in my dreams
                  And in places like the Eifel Tower
                  And the Louvre.
                    Floating in the Alaskan seas
                    And the Caribbean.
                      Broadway and Zabars
                      And strolling along the Bay!!

I never tire of saying it.
  For every time I say it
    I become peaceful and serene
      And the feeling in my heart and in my soul
        Is like no other feeling I know.

My heart never knew that it was possible to want to be
  With someone for the rest of eternity and more.
    I never knew the real meaning of this word until
      I met you and then my life began. My being and
        My soul came together and merged with yours.

The "it" is a word I tell you all of the time. The
  Word is LOVE. Love is the only word I know that
    Brings with it commitment, liking, devotion,
      Attachment, affection, ardor, fondness, passion,
        Tenderness and caring and the deepest most
          Wonderful friendship I have ever known.

The kind of love we have is like the most beautiful
  Flower in the world. It could not exist if it wasn't
    Cared for and nurtured and given everything that
      It needs to remain alive and to rise above
        Life itself.

Happy Birthday, dearest. We will celebrate many more!

I LOVE YOU WITH ALL MY HEART!
          KEN

To My Dearest and Most Wonderful
ROSE
Mine BatMitzvah Girl!!!

On this very Wondrous Day in May
You Make My Heart Sing,
In a Very Special Way
Of a New Kind of Love
For You!!!

You are Magical
THIRTEEN!!!!
You Changed Your Age From Seventy Six to
Right In Front of My Very Eyes!
I Have Watched You, Lo These Many Years,
And I have Always Been Surprised and Amazed
By Your Fabulous Accomplishments!!!

You Do What You Say
You Are Going To Do
And
You Do It
With Care, Love and Integrity!!
Even When There is The Fear of
Not Knowing Where You Are Going!!!
You Go Anyway and I Love You For It!!!

Now, On This Day in May,
You Have Done a Mitzvah
For You, For Me and For All of
Your Family, Friends and Clients!
YOU ARE THE GREATEST!!!!

Awakening

Come to me, my Love –
    It's time.
The Wee hours of solitude
    are over.
Come to me, my Love –
    Dawn's urge to be
      Near you
        is like
          Sunrise.

Come to me, my Love –
    Nestle soul and body
      within my arms,
        So that I may feel
          The sheer joy
            of your yielding flesh
            upon my own.

Come to me, my Love –
    I want so to caress you
      to kiss your eyes with mine.
        Let the dawn light awaken you slowly.
        Hear me whisper,
          I love you,
            as an unceasing melody,
            Intermingled with
              my touch.
                Let love – My love
                  Make full your Response.
                  Now let the
                    Sun Light In!

Eyelight Poems was edited by
Rebecca Salome, publisher of Manto Press
in Berkeley, California.
Harrison Shaffer designed the layout and set
the type in 11 pt. Granjon with Kabel display.

This book was published by
Whitewing Press
an imprint of Green Sand Press
Tucson, Arizona 85728-5539

www.greensand.org